Contents

W9-CPF-815

Chile 'n' Cheese Spirals

4 ounces cream cheese, softened
1 cup (4 ounces) shredded cheddar cheese
1 can (4 ounces) ORTEGA Diced Green Chiles
3 green onions, sliced
½ cup chopped red bell pepper
1 can (2.25 ounces) chopped ripe olives
4 (8-inch) taco-size flour tortillas
ORTEGA Salsa, any variety

COMBINE cream cheese, cheddar cheese, chiles, green onions, pepper and olives in medium bowl.

SPREAD ½ cup cheese mixture on each tortilla; roll up. Wrap each roll in plastic wrap; chill for 1 hour.

REMOVE plastic wrap; slice each roll into six ¾-inch pieces. Serve with salsa for dipping.   *Makes 24 appetizers*

Tip: Chili 'n' Cheese Spirals can be made ahead and kept in the refrigerator for 1 to 2 days.

Ortega® 7-Layer Dip

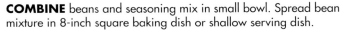

1 can (16 ounces) **ORTEGA Refried Beans**
1 package (1.25 ounces) **ORTEGA Taco Seasoning Mix**
1 container (8 ounces) **sour cream**
1 container (8 ounces) **refrigerated guacamole**
1 cup (4 ounces) **shredded cheddar cheese**
1 cup **ORTEGA Salsa, any variety**
1 can (4 ounces) **ORTEGA Diced Green Chiles**
2 large green onions, sliced
   Tortilla chips

COMBINE beans and seasoning mix in small bowl. Spread bean mixture in 8-inch square baking dish or shallow serving dish.

TOP with sour cream, guacamole, cheese, salsa, chiles and green onions. Serve with chips. *Makes 10 to 12 servings*

Tip: Can be prepared and refrigerated up to 2 hours before serving.

Nachos à la Ortega®

1 can (16 ounces) ORTEGA Refried Beans, warmed
4 cups baked tortilla chips
1½ cups (6 ounces) shredded Monterey Jack cheese
2 tablespoons ORTEGA Sliced Jalapeños

Suggested Toppings
ORTEGA Salsa-Thick & Chunky, sour cream, guacamole,
sliced ripe olives, chopped green onions, chopped fresh
cilantro

PREHEAT broiler.

SPREAD beans over bottom of large ovenproof platter. Arrange chips over beans. Top with cheese and jalapeños.

BROIL for 1 to 1½ minutes or until cheese is melted. Top with desired toppings. *Makes 4 to 6 servings*

Smokey Chipotle Party Dip

¾ **cup sour cream**
¾ **cup mayonnaise**
¾ **cup ORTEGA Salsa, any variety**
1 **package (1.25 ounces) ORTEGA Smokey Chipotle Taco Seasoning Mix**
Chopped tomatoes, chopped cilantro, chopped ripe olives and shredded cheddar cheese
Blue corn tortilla chips

COMBINE sour cream, mayonnaise, salsa and seasoning mix; stir until blended.

SPREAD dip in shallow serving dish or pie plate and sprinkle with tomatoes, cilantro, olives and cheese. Serve with tortilla chips.

Makes 2¼ cups dip

Tip: This flavorful dip is ready to go as soon as you make it, but can also be prepared and refrigerated up to 2 days before serving.

Mexican Pizza

1 pound ground beef
¾ cup water
1 package (1.25 ounces) ORTEGA Taco Seasoning Mix
1 can (16 ounces) ORTEGA Refried Beans, divided
1 package (10) ORTEGA Tostada Shells
2½ cups shredded Nacho & Taco blend cheese, divided

Suggested Toppings
   Shredded lettuce, chopped tomatoes, sliced ripe olives,
      sliced avocado, chopped cilantro, sliced green onions,
      sour cream, guacamole, whole kernel corn, ORTEGA
      Salsa-Thick & Chunky

BROWN beef; drain. Stir in water and seasoning mix. Bring to a boil. Reduce heat to low; cook, stirring occasionally, for 5 to 6 minutes or until mixture is thickened.

SPREAD 2 tablespoons beans on each tostada shell. Top with about ¼ cup meat mixture and ¼ cup cheese. Broil for 1 to 2 minutes or until cheese is melted. Garnish with desired toppings.

Makes 10 servings

Ortega® Green Chile Guacamole

2 medium very ripe avocados, seeded, peeled and mashed
1 can (4 ounces) ORTEGA Diced Green Chiles
2 large green onions, chopped
2 tablespoons olive oil
1 teaspoon lime juice
1 clove garlic, finely chopped
¼ teaspoon salt
  Tortilla chips

COMBINE avocados, chiles, green onions, olive oil, lime juice, garlic and salt in medium bowl. Cover; refrigerate for at least 1 hour. Serve with chips.   *Makes 2 cups*

Note: This all-time favorite dip can be used in tacos, burritos, tamales, chimichangas or combined with ORTEGA Salsa for a spicy salad dressing.

Bandito Buffalo Wings

1 package (1.25 ounces) ORTEGA Taco Seasoning Mix
12 (about 1 pound total) chicken wings
  ORTEGA Salsa, any variety

PREHEAT oven to 375°F. Lightly grease 13×9-inch baking pan.

PLACE seasoning mix in heavy-duty plastic or paper bag. Add 3 chicken wings; shake well to coat. Place wings in prepared pan. Repeat until all wings have been coated.

BAKE for 35 to 40 minutes or until juices run clear. Serve with salsa for dipping.   *Makes 6 appetizer servings*

Chili-Chicken Enchiladas

Nonstick cooking spray
3 cups (12 ounces) shredded cheddar
and/or Monterey Jack cheese, divided
1½ cups sour cream, divided
¾ cup roasted red peppers, drained and chopped, divided
1 can (7 ounces) ORTEGA Diced Green Chiles, divided
2 cups diced cooked chicken
1 can (10 ounces) ORTEGA Enchilada Sauce
8 (8-inch) ORTEGA Soft Flour Tortillas

PREHEAT oven to 350°F. Spray 13×9-inch glass baking dish with cooking spray. Reserve 1½ cups cheese, ½ cup sour cream and ¼ cup each red peppers and green chiles; set aside.

MIX chicken with remaining cheese, sour cream, red peppers and green chiles in medium bowl.

SPREAD about 2 teaspoons enchilada sauce over each tortilla. Top each with about ½ cup chicken mixture. Roll up tortillas; arrange, seam side down, in baking dish. Top tortillas with remaining enchilada sauce. Sprinkle with the reserved cheese.

COVER with foil. Bake for 50 to 60 minutes or until hot, removing foil during last 5 minutes of baking time.

SPOON reserved sour cream over top and sprinkle with the reserved red peppers and green chiles.

Makes 4 servings (2 enchiladas each)

Tip: If you can't find a 7-ounce can of ORTEGA Diced Green Chiles, use two 4-ounce cans.

Mexican Steak Tacos

1 (3.5-ounce) boil-in-bag long-grain rice
1 tablespoon ORTEGA Salsa, any variety
2 teaspoons ground cumin
1 teaspoon garlic powder
1 teaspoon ORTEGA Taco Sauce
¼ teaspoon salt
1 pound sirloin steak
   Nonstick cooking spray
1 can (about 14 ounces) diced tomatoes
1 can (4 ounces) ORTEGA Diced Green Chiles
1 package (12) ORTEGA Taco Shells
12 lime wedges and sour cream (optional)

COOK rice. Combine salsa, cumin, garlic powder, taco sauce and salt. Rub mixture over both sides of steak. Spray broiler pan with cooking spray. Place steak on pan. Broil steak for 4 minutes on each side or until desired degree of doneness. Cut steak into thin slices.

COMBINE rice, tomatoes and chiles in small pan; cook over medium heat until hot. Place mixture in shells. Top with beef. Squeeze lime juice over beef. Top with sour cream, if desired.   *Makes 12 tacos*

Refried Bean Tostadas

- 1 can (16 ounces) **ORTEGA Refried Beans**
- ¼ cup chopped onion
- 1 package (1.25 ounces) **ORTEGA Taco Seasoning Mix**
- 1 package (10) **ORTEGA Tostada Shells, warmed**
- 2 cups shredded lettuce
- ½ cup (2 ounces) shredded cheddar cheese
- ⅓ cup sliced ripe olives
- 2 medium ripe avocados, cut into 20 slices
- ¾ cup **ORTEGA Thick & Smooth Taco Sauce**

COMBINE beans, onion and seasoning mix in medium saucepan. Cook, stirring frequently, for 4 to 5 minutes or until heated through.

SPREAD about ¼ cup bean mixture over each shell. Top with lettuce, cheese, olives, avocado and taco sauce.   *Makes 10 tostadas*

Baja Fish Tacos

½ **cup sour cream**
½ **cup mayonnaise**
¼ **cup chopped fresh cilantro**
1 **package (1.25 ounces) ORTEGA Taco Seasoning Mix, divided**
1 **pound cod or other white fish fillets, cut into 1-inch pieces**
2 **tablespoons vegetable oil**
2 **tablespoons lemon juice**
1 **package (12) ORTEGA Taco Shells**
   Toppings: shredded cabbage, chopped tomato, lime juice, ORTEGA Taco Sauce

COMBINE sour cream, mayonnaise, cilantro and 2 tablespoons taco seasoning mix in small bowl.

COMBINE cod, vegetable oil, lemon juice and remaining taco seasoning mix in medium bowl; pour into large skillet. Cook, stirring constantly, over medium-high heat for 4 to 5 minutes or until fish flakes easily when tested with fork.

FILL taco shells with fish mixture. Layer with desired toppings. Top with sour cream sauce.   *Makes 12 tacos*

Breakfast Burritos

½ pound (8 ounces) ground sausage
1 large potato, peeled and grated
1 package (8-inch) ORTEGA Soft Flour Tortillas
4 eggs
1 jar (16 ounces) ORTEGA Salsa, any variety
1 can (4 ounces) ORTEGA Diced Green Chiles
1 large tomato, diced
½ cup grated cheddar cheese
  Salt and black pepper

COOK sausage in large skillet over medium-high heat; add potatoes. Cook until brown. Drain fat.

WARM tortillas according to package directions. Cook and scramble eggs.

DIVIDE eggs, sausage mixture, salsa, chiles, tomato and cheese evenly among tortillas. Season to taste with salt and pepper.

FOLD tortillas and serve immediately. Top with additional salsa, if desired.   *Makes 2 servings*

Chicken and Black Bean Soft Tacos

1 package (15.2 ounces) ORTEGA Soft Taco Kit
1 tablespoon vegetable oil
1 pound (3 to 4) boneless, skinless chicken breast halves,
cut into 2-inch strips
1 medium onion, chopped
1 can (about 15 ounces) black beans, rinsed and drained
¾ cup whole kernel corn
½ cup water
2 tablespoons lime juice

HEAT oil in large skillet over medium-high heat. Add chicken and onion; cook 4 to 5 minutes or until chicken is no longer pink in center. Stir in taco seasoning mix from kit, beans, corn, water and lime juice. Bring to a boil. Reduce heat to low; cook, stirring occasionally, 5 to 6 minutes or until mixture is thickened.

REMOVE tortillas from outer plastic pouch. Microwave on HIGH (100%) 10 to 15 seconds or until warm. Fill each tortilla with ½ cup chicken mixture. Serve with taco sauce from kit.   *Makes 10 tacos*

Tortilla Scramble with Salsa

8 eggs
¼ cup heavy whipping cream or half and half
1 tablespoon butter
3 tablespoons ORTEGA Salsa, any variety
1 cup broken ORTEGA Taco Shells
½ cup (2 ounces) shredded cheddar cheese
   Tortilla chips, chopped parsley and salsa (optional)

COMBINE eggs and heavy cream in mixing bowl. Beat with wire whisk.

MELT butter in heavy skillet. Add egg mixture and stir in 3 tablespoons salsa. Scramble eggs until they begin to set. Add broken taco shells and cheese, stirring to mix.

DIVIDE egg mixture evenly among individual plates.

TOP with tortilla chips, parsley and salsa, if desired.

Makes 4 servings

Original Ortega® Taco Recipe

1 pound ground beef
1 package (1.25 ounces) ORTEGA Taco Seasoning Mix
¾ cup water
1 package (12) ORTEGA Taco Shells, warmed

Suggested Toppings
    Shredded lettuce, chopped tomatoes, shredded cheddar cheese, ORTEGA Thick & Smooth Taco Sauce

BROWN beef; drain. Stir in seasoning mix and water; bring to a boil. Reduce heat to low; cook, stirring occasionally, for 5 to 6 minutes or until mixture is thickened.

FILL taco shells with beef mixture. Top with desired toppings.

Makes 12 tacos

Bean and Cheese Burritos

1 can (16 ounces) ORTEGA Refried Beans
1 cup chopped red onion
1 can (4 ounces) ORTEGA Diced Green Chiles
1 package (1.25 ounces) ORTEGA Burrito Seasoning
2 tablespoons lime juice
1 teaspoon minced garlic
½ teaspoon ground cumin
4 (8-inch) ORTEGA Soft Flour Tortillas
4 tablespoons shredded cheddar cheese
    Nonstick cooking spray
    ORTEGA Salsa, any variety, and sour cream

PREHEAT oven to 400°F. Prepare filling by mixing beans, onion, chiles, burrito seasoning, lime juice, garlic and cumin.

ASSEMBLE burrito by spooning ½ cup bean filling into center of each tortilla and top with 1 tablespoon cheddar cheese. Fold in ends, and then sides. Place burritos seam side down on baking sheet that has been sprayed with cooking spray. Bake for 20 to 25 minutes until golden brown. Serve with salsa and sour cream.   *Makes 4 burritos*

Breakfast Nachos

1 can (16 ounces) **ORTEGA Refried Beans, heated**
4 cups (4 ounces) **tortilla chips**
4 eggs, scrambled until fully cooked
1½ cups (6 ounces) **shredded cheddar or Monterey Jack cheese**
¼ cup **ORTEGA Sliced Jalapeños**

Suggested Toppings
ORTEGA Salsa-Thick & Chunky, sour cream, guacamole, chopped green onions, chopped fresh cilantro, sliced ripe olives, cooked crumbled sausage

PREHEAT broiler.

SPREAD beans onto bottom of large ovenproof platter or jelly-roll pan; arrange chips over beans. Top with eggs, cheese and jalapeños.

PLACE under preheated broiler, 4 inches away from heat source, for 1 to 1½ minutes or until cheese is melted. Top with desired toppings.

Makes 4 to 6 servings

Spicy Chicken Tortilla Casserole

- **1 tablespoon vegetable oil**
- **1 cup chopped green bell pepper**
- **1 small onion, chopped**
- **2 cloves garlic, finely chopped**
- **1 pound (3 to 4) boneless, skinless chicken breast halves,
  cut into bite-size pieces**
- **1 jar (16 ounces) ORTEGA Salsa, any variety**
- **1 can (2.25 ounces) sliced ripe olives**
- **6 corn tortillas, cut into halves**
- **2 cups (8 ounces) shredded Monterey Jack or cheddar cheese
  Sour cream (optional)**

PREHEAT oven to 350°F. Heat oil in large skillet over medium-high heat. Add bell pepper, onion and garlic; cook for 2 to 3 minutes or until vegetables are tender. Add chicken; cook, stirring frequently, for 3 to 5 minutes or until chicken is no longer pink in center. Stir in salsa and olives; remove from heat.

PLACE 6 tortilla halves onto bottom of ungreased 8-inch square baking pan. Top with half of chicken mixture and 1 cup cheese; repeat. Bake for 15 to 20 minutes or until bubbly. Serve with sour cream.

Makes 8 servings

Stuffed Pork Tenderloin with Cilantro-Lime Pesto

1 to 1 1/2 pounds pork tenderloin
1/2 onion, cut into chunks
1/2 cup lightly packed fresh cilantro
2 tablespoons lime juice
3 large cloves garlic, peeled
1 teaspoon ORTEGA Diced Jalapeños
2 tablespoons corn oil
1/2 cup (2 ounces) shredded Monterey Jack
**   or crumbled Cotija cheese**
**   ORTEGA Salsa-Thick and Chunky**

PREHEAT oven to 400°F.

CUT tenderloin lengthwise almost in half. Open; lay flat between two pieces of waxed paper. Pound with meat mallet or rolling pin to 1/2-inch thickness.

PLACE onion, cilantro, lime juice, garlic and jalapeños in food processor or blender container; cover. Process until coarsely chopped. Process, while slowly adding oil, for 10 to 15 seconds or until mixture is almost smooth. Spread half of cilantro mixture over tenderloin; top with cheese. Roll up; tie with cotton string. Spread remaining cilantro mixture over top. Place on rack in roasting pan.

BAKE for 55 to 60 minutes or until internal temperature of 160°F is reached. Cool in pan on wire rack for 5 minutes. Remove string; slice. Serve with salsa.   *Makes 4 servings*

Note: Ladle salsa onto bottom of plate and top with tenderloin slices for a fantastic presentation!

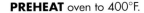

Santa Fe Fish Fillets with Mango-Cilantro Salsa

Nonstick cooking spray
1½ pounds fish fillets (cod, perch or tilapia, about ½-inch thick)
½ package (3 tablespoons) ORTEGA Taco Seasoning Mix
3 ORTEGA Taco Shells (white or corn), finely crushed
1 cup ORTEGA Salsa, any variety
½ cup diced mango
2 tablespoons chopped cilantro

PREHEAT oven to 375°F. Cover broiler pan with foil. Spray with cooking spray.

DIP fish fillets in taco seasoning mix, coating both sides; place on foil. Spray coated fillets with cooking spray. Sprinkle with crushed taco shells. Bake 15 to 20 minutes until flaky in center.

MICROWAVE salsa on HIGH (100%) 1 minute. Stir in mango and cilantro. Spoon salsa over fish. *Makes 4 to 6 servings*

Note: Refrigerated jars of sliced mango can be found in the produce section at most supermarkets.

Mexican Omelette

4 eggs
¼ cup half and half
1 teaspoon dried oregano
½ teaspoon salt
⅛ teaspoon pepper
2 tablespoons butter or margarine
1 container (13 ounces) ORTEGA Salsa & Cheese Bowl
¼ cup ORTEGA Diced Green Chiles
   Chopped tomatoes, sour cream and chopped cilantro

MIX eggs, half and half, oregano and salt and pepper with fork.

COAT heated pan with butter. Add egg mixture and spread over bottom of pan. When egg mixture thickens, spread with Salsa & Cheese and chiles. Fold over.

TOP omelette with tomatoes, sour cream and cilantro.

Makes 2 servings

Taco Topped Baked Potato

4 large baking potatoes, scrubbed
½ pound (8 ounces) ground beef
¼ cup chopped onion
1 package (1.25 ounces) ORTEGA Taco Seasoning Mix
1 container (13 ounces) ORTEGA Salsa & Cheese Bowl
Sour cream (optional)

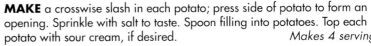

PRICK potatoes several times with a fork. Microwave on HIGH (100%) uncovered, 12 to 15 minutes or until just tender, turning potatoes over and re-arranging once.

CRUMBLE ground beef into 1 quart glass casserole; add onion. Microwave on HIGH (100%) uncovered, 3 to 3½ minutes or until meat is set, stirring once; drain. Stir in taco seasoning and half the amount of water specified on taco seasoning package. Add contents of Salsa & Cheese Bowl. Cover; microwave on HIGH (100%) 2½ to 3 minutes or until heated through, stirring once.

MAKE a crosswise slash in each potato; press side of potato to form an opening. Sprinkle with salt to taste. Spoon filling into potatoes. Top each potato with sour cream, if desired. *Makes 4 servings*

Arroz con Pollo

4 slices bacon
1½ pounds (about 6) boneless, skinless chicken breasts
1 cup (1 small) chopped onion
1 cup (1 small) chopped green bell pepper
2 large cloves garlic, finely chopped
2 cups uncooked long-grain white rice
1 jar (16 ounces) ORTEGA Salsa, any variety
1¾ cups (14½-ounce can) chicken broth
1 cup (8-ounce can) tomato sauce
1 teaspoon salt
½ teaspoon ground cumin
Chopped parsley

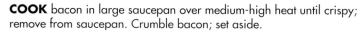

COOK bacon in large saucepan over medium-high heat until crispy; remove from saucepan. Crumble bacon; set aside.

ADD chicken to saucepan; cook, turning frequently, for 5 to 7 minutes or until golden on both sides. Remove from saucepan; keep warm. Discard all but 2 tablespoons drippings from saucepan.

ADD onion, bell pepper and garlic; cook for 3 to 4 minutes or until crisp-tender. Add rice; cook for 2 to 3 minutes. Stir in salsa, chicken broth, tomato sauce, salt and cumin. Bring to a boil. Place chicken over rice mixture; reduce heat to low. Cover.

COOK for 20 to 25 minutes or until most of moisture is absorbed and chicken is no longer pink in center. Sprinkle with bacon and parsley.

Makes 6 servings

Spicy Skillet Vegetables, Salsa-Style

2 cups finely diced peeled potatoes
½ cup water
2 tablespoons vegetable oil
1 green bell pepper, cut into strips
1 red bell pepper, cut into strips
1 jar (16 ounces) ORTEGA Salsa, any variety
1 can (about 15 ounces) black beans, rinsed and drained
1 can (15 ounces) corn, drained
¼ cup ORTEGA Diced Jalapeños
1 cup (4 ounces) crumbled queso fresco or shredded Monterey Jack cheese

MICROWAVE potatoes with water, covered, on HIGH (100%) 5 minutes. Drain. Meanwhile, in large skillet, heat oil over medium-high heat.

COOK and stir bell pepper strips in skillet for 3 to 4 minutes. Stir in drained potatoes and salsa, then beans, corn and jalapeños.

BRING to a boil. Cover; reduce heat to medium and cook for 5 minutes, or until potatoes are tender.

SPRINKLE with cheese before serving.

Makes 8 servings (1 cup each)

Note: If jalapeños are too hot for your family, use diced green chiles instead.

Mexican Hash Brown Bake

Nonstick cooking spray
1 container (13 ounces) ORTEGA Salsa & Cheese Bowl
1½ cups sour cream
1 can (4 ounces) ORTEGA Diced Green Chiles or Diced Jalapeños
1 package (30 ounces) frozen shredded hash brown potatoes
2 ORTEGA Taco Shells, coarsely crushed

PREHEAT oven to 350°F. Spray 13×9-inch baking dish with cooking spray.

COMBINE Salsa & Cheese, sour cream and chiles in large bowl; stir until blended. Gently stir in hash browns. Spoon mixture into baking dish.

SPRINKLE with crushed taco shells.

BAKE for 45 to 50 minutes or until bubbly around edges. Let stand for 5 minutes before serving. *Makes 12 servings (1 cup each)*

Note: Make this dish extra special by topping with sliced green onions or crisp, crumbled bacon.

Veggie-Pepper Bowl with Rice

8 medium green bell peppers, halved and seeded
3 cups cooked long-grain white rice
1 package (10 ounces) frozen peas and carrots
1 cup whole kernel corn
½ cup chopped green onions
1¾ cups ORTEGA Salsa, any variety, divided
1½ cups 4-cheese Mexican blend, divided

PREHEAT oven to 375°F. Place bell peppers in microwave-safe dish with 3 tablespoons water. Cover with plastic wrap. Microwave on HIGH (100%) for 4 to 5 minutes or until slightly tender. Drain.

COMBINE rice, peas and carrots, corn, green onions, ¾ cup salsa and 1 cup cheese in large bowl. Fill each pepper with about ½ cup rice mixture. Place peppers in ungreased 13×9-inch baking dish; top with remaining salsa and cheese.

BAKE, covered, for 20 to 25 minutes. Uncover; bake for additional 5 minutes or until heated through and cheese is melted.

Makes 8 servings

South-of-the-Border Rice and Beans

1 ¼ cups water
1 cup ORTEGA Salsa, any variety
½ package (3 tablespoons) ORTEGA Taco Seasoning Mix
2 teaspoons vegetable oil
2 cups uncooked instant white rice
1 can (about 15 ounces) pinto beans, drained and rinsed
¼ cup chopped cilantro

COMBINE water, salsa, seasoning mix and oil in large saucepan; mix well. Stir in rice and beans; mix well.

BRING to a boil over medium-high heat. Cover; remove from heat. Let stand 5 minutes.

STIR in cilantro.   *Makes 4 servings*

Note: Serve this side dish with grilled chicken or pork. Brush the meat with oil and sprinkle with extra taco seasoning mix for a flavorful entrée.

Fiesta-Style Roasted Vegetables

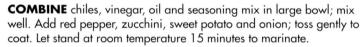

1 can (4 ounces) **ORTEGA** Diced Green Chiles
3 tablespoons vinegar
2 tablespoons vegetable oil
1 package (1.25 ounces) **ORTEGA** Taco Seasoning Mix
1 small red bell pepper, cut into strips
1 medium zucchini, cut into ½-inch slices
1 small sweet potato, peeled, cut into ⅛-inch slices and halved
1 small red onion, cut into wedges
   Nonstick cooking spray

COMBINE chiles, vinegar, oil and seasoning mix in large bowl; mix well. Add red pepper, zucchini, sweet potato and onion; toss gently to coat. Let stand at room temperature 15 minutes to marinate.

PREHEAT oven to 450°F. Cover 15×10-inch baking pan with foil and spray with cooking spray.

REMOVE vegetables from marinade with spoon, placing on prepared pan. Bake 20 to 25 minutes until tender and browned, stirring once.

Makes 4 servings

Black & White Mexican Bean Soup

1 tablespoon vegetable oil
1 cup chopped onion
1 clove garlic, minced
¼ cup flour
1 package (1.25 ounces) ORTEGA Taco Seasoning Mix
2 cups milk
1 can (about 14 ounces) chicken broth
1 package (16 ounces) frozen corn
1 can (about 15 ounces) great northern beans,
    rinsed and drained
1 can (about 15 ounces) black beans, rinsed and drained
1 can (4 ounces) ORTEGA Diced Green Chiles
2 tablespoons chopped cilantro

HEAT oil in large pan or Dutch oven over medium-high heat. Add onion and garlic; cook until onion is tender.

STIR in flour and taco seasoning mix; gradually stir in milk until blended. Add remaining ingredients except cilantro.

BRING to a boil, stirring constantly. Reduce heat to low; simmer for 15 minutes or until thickened, stirring occasionally.

STIR in cilantro. *Makes 6 servings*

Tip: To save time, substitute ½ teaspoon bottled minced garlic for garlic clove.

Crunchy Mexican Side Salad

3 cups romaine and iceberg lettuce blend
½ cup grape tomatoes, halved
½ cup peeled and diced jicama
¼ cup sliced ripe olives
¼ cup ORTEGA Sliced Jalapeños, quartered
2 tablespoons ORTEGA Taco Sauce
1 tablespoon vegetable oil
⅛ teaspoon salt
  Crushed ORTEGA Taco Shells (optional)

TOSS together lettuce, tomatoes, jicama, olives and jalapeños in large bowl.

COMBINE taco sauce, oil and salt in small bowl. Stir with a fork until blended.

POUR dressing over salad; toss gently to coat. Top with taco shells, if desired. *Makes 4 servings*

Note: ORTEGA Sliced Jalapeños are available in a 12-ounce jar. They are pickled, adding great flavor and crunch to this salad.

Chili con Carne

- **2 tablespoons vegetable oil**
- **2 pounds ground beef**
- **2 cups chopped onions**
- **4 cloves garlic, finely chopped**
- **2 cans (15 ounces each) kidney, pinto or black beans, drained**
- **1 can (28 ounces) crushed tomatoes**
- **1 jar (16 ounces) ORTEGA Salsa-Thick & Chunky**
- **½ cup dry white wine**
- **1 can (4 ounces) ORTEGA Diced Green Chiles**
- **3 tablespoons chili powder**
- **1 to 2 tablespoons ORTEGA Diced Jalapeños**
- **1 tablespoon ground cumin**
- **1 tablespoon dried oregano, crushed**
- **2 teaspoons salt**

HEAT vegetable oil in large saucepan over medium-high heat. Add beef, onions and garlic; cook for 4 to 5 minutes or until no longer pink; drain.

STIR in beans, tomatoes, salsa, wine, chiles, chili powder, jalapeños, cumin, oregano and salt. Bring to a boil. Reduce heat to low; cover. Cook, stirring occasionally, for 1 hour.   *Makes 10 to 12 servings*

Chopped Salad Tostadas

1 package (10) ORTEGA Tostada Shells
6 cups shredded iceberg lettuce
1 cup shredded carrot
1 can (2.25 ounces) chopped ripe olives
1 tomato, seeded, chopped and drained
⅓ cup ranch dressing
6 tablespoons ORTEGA Taco Sauce, divided
1 can (16 ounces) ORTEGA Refried Beans
10 tablespoons shredded Mexican blend cheese

HEAT tostada shells according to package directions. Meanwhile, in large bowl, gently toss lettuce, carrot, olives and tomato.

MIX ranch dressing and 2 tablespoons taco sauce in small bowl. Pour dressing over lettuce mixture; toss gently to coat.

COMBINE refried beans and remaining 4 tablespoons taco sauce in saucepan; heat over medium heat until warm.

SPREAD each tostada shell with 3 tablespoons bean mixture; top with about ¾ cup salad mixture and sprinkle with cheese.

Makes 10 tostadas

Mexican Pasta Salad

3 cups (8 ounces) uncooked rotini pasta
½ cup sour cream
1 package (1.25 ounces) ORTEGA Taco Seasoning Mix
¼ cup water
1 tablespoon vinegar
1 cup cherry tomato halves
1 can (4 ounces) ORTEGA Diced Green Chiles
½ cup diced green bell pepper
1 can (2.25 ounces) sliced ripe olives, drained
2 green onions, sliced
2 ORTEGA Taco Shells, coarsely crushed
½ cup ORTEGA Salsa, any variety
½ cup (2 ounces) shredded cheddar cheese

COOK pasta according to package directions (do not overcook); drain. Rinse with cold water until cooled; drain.

STIR together sour cream, taco seasoning mix, water and vinegar in large bowl until blended. Stir in pasta, cherry tomatoes, green chiles, bell pepper, olives and green onions.

MICROWAVE crushed taco shells on HIGH (100%) 30 to 45 seconds.

PLACE pasta in serving bowls. Top with salsa, crushed taco shells and cheese just before serving.   *Makes 8 servings*

Tip: Stir in a little water for a creamier salad.

South-of-the Border Salad with Creamy Lime Dressing

Creamy Lime Dressing
- ⅓ **cup sour cream**
- **3 tablespoons chopped cilantro**
- **2 tablespoons lime juice**
- **1 tablespoon** *each* **vegetable oil and milk**
- ¼ **teaspoon salt**

Salad
- **4 ORTEGA Taco Shells, crushed**
- **2 tablespoons vegetable oil**
- **1 pound boneless chicken breasts, cut into strips**
- **1 package (1.25 ounces) ORTEGA Taco Seasoning Mix**
- ¾ **cup water**
- **1 package (5 ounces) mixed salad greens**
- **1 cup cherry tomato halves**
- ½ **cup ORTEGA Sliced Jalapeños, coarsely chopped**
- ½ **cup (2 ounces) shredded Cheddar & Monterey Jack cheese**
- **1 avocado, pitted, peeled, sliced and sprinkled with lime juice**

COMBINE all Creamy Lime Dressing ingredients in small bowl; stir until blended.

MICROWAVE crushed taco shells on HIGH (100%) 30 to 45 seconds.

HEAT oil in large skillet over medium-high heat. Add chicken strips; cook and stir 4 to 6 minutes or until chicken is no longer pink. Stir in taco seasoning mix and water. Bring to a boil. Reduce heat to low; cook for 2 to 3 minutes or until mixture is thickened, stirring occasionally. Remove from heat.

COMBINE salad greens, crushed taco shells, tomatoes and jalapeños in large bowl. Divide mixture onto four serving plates.

SPRINKLE each salad with cheese; top with chicken strips and avocado slices.

SERVE with Creamy Lime Dressing.   *Makes 4 servings*

Cheesy Mexican Soup

1 cup chopped onion
1 tablespoon vegetable oil
1 container (13 ounces) ORTEGA Salsa & Cheese Bowl
2 cups milk
1 can (about 14 ounces) chicken broth
1 can (7 ounces) ORTEGA Diced Green Chiles
4 ORTEGA Taco Shells, crushed
¼ cup chopped cilantro

COOK and stir onion in oil in large saucepan over medium-high heat for 4 to 6 minutes until tender. Reduce heat to medium-low.

STIR in Salsa & Cheese, milk, chicken broth and green chiles; cook for 5 to 7 minutes until hot, stirring frequently.

MICROWAVE crushed taco shells on HIGH (100%) 30 to 45 seconds. Cool. Serve soup sprinkled with cilantro and crushed taco shells.

Makes 8 servings

Tip: If you can't find a 7-ounce can of ORTEGA Diced Green Chiles, use two 4-ounce cans.

Mexican Taco Salad

1 pound ground beef or turkey
1 cup chopped onion
1 cup **ORTEGA Salsa-Thick & Chunky**
¾ cup water
1 package (1.25 ounces) **ORTEGA Taco Seasoning Mix**
1 can (about 15 ounces) kidney or pinto beans,
    rinsed and drained
1 can (4 ounces) **ORTEGA Diced Green Chiles**
3 cups tortilla chips *or* 6 taco shells, broken into large pieces
6 cups shredded lettuce, divided
¾ cup (3 ounces) shredded Nacho & Taco blend cheese,
    divided

Suggested Toppings
    Sour cream, guacamole, **ORTEGA Thick & Smooth Taco Sauce**

COOK beef and onion in large skillet over medium high heat until beef is brown; drain. Stir in salsa, water and seasoning mix. Bring to a boil. Reduce heat to low; cook for 2 to 3 minutes. Stir in beans and chiles.

LAYER ingredients as follows on ½ cup chips: 1 cup lettuce, ¾ cup meat mixture, 2 tablespoons cheese and desired toppings.

Makes 6 servings

Chicken Taco Salad Wraps

- **1 ripe large avocado, pitted, peeled and diced**
- **¾ cup peeled and diced jicama**
- **2 teaspoons lime juice**
- **2 tablespoons vegetable oil**
- **1 pound boneless chicken breasts, cut into strips**
- **1 package (1.25 ounces) ORTEGA Taco Seasoning Mix**
- **¾ cup water**
- **8 ORTEGA Taco Shells, coarsely crushed**
- **12 large Bibb lettuce leaves**
- **½ cup (2 ounces) shredded Mexican blend cheese**
- **¼ cup chopped fresh cilantro**
- **1 jar (8 ounces) ORTEGA Taco Sauce**

STIR together avocado and jicama with lime juice in small bowl; set aside. Heat oil in large skillet over medium-high heat. Add chicken; cook and stir 4 to 6 minutes or until chicken is no longer pink. Stir in taco seasoning mix and water. Bring to a boil. Reduce heat to low; cook for 2 to 3 minutes or until mixture is thickened, stirring occasionally.

MICROWAVE crushed taco shells on HIGH (100%) 1 minute. Spoon ⅓ cup chicken filling onto each lettuce leaf; layer with taco shells, avocado mixture, cheese and cilantro. Wrap lettuce around filling and serve with taco sauce.   *Makes 4 servings (3 wraps each)*

Smokey Chipotle Salad

1 package (15.2 ounces) **ORTEGA Soft Taco Kit**
2 tablespoons vegetable oil
¼ cup sour cream
3 tablespoons mayonnaise
2 chipotle chiles in adobo sauce, seeded and finely chopped
1 pound ground beef
1 bag (15 ounces) romaine salad mix
1 cup (4 ounces) shredded Cheddar & Monterey Jack cheese
1 can (2.25 ounces) sliced ripe olives, drained

HEAT oven to 400°F. Brush each tortilla from Soft Taco Kit with ¼ teaspoon oil; cut into fourths. Place on 2 baking sheets. Bake 5 to 7 minutes, or until lightly browned. Prepare dressing by combining sour cream, mayonnaise, chipotle chiles and taco sauce from kit; stir until blended. Cook ground beef as directed on Soft Taco Kit using seasoning mix from kit. Toss romaine with dressing in large bowl until lightly coated.

ASSEMBLE each salad onto serving plates by layering 1½ cups romaine mixture, ⅔ cup beef mixture, 3 tablespoons cheese and 1½ tablespoons olives. Serve each salad with tortilla pieces.

Makes 4 to 5 servings